Let's Learn American Sign Language

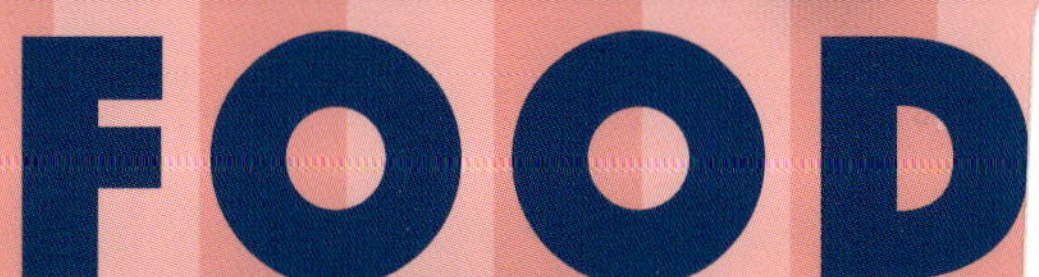

Raymie Davis

Illustrations By:
Brad Manker,
35 Corks Art Studio

PowerKiDS press.

PK Beginners

I can sign about food.
I use my hands.

"FOOD"

milk

juice

cheese

cracker

apple

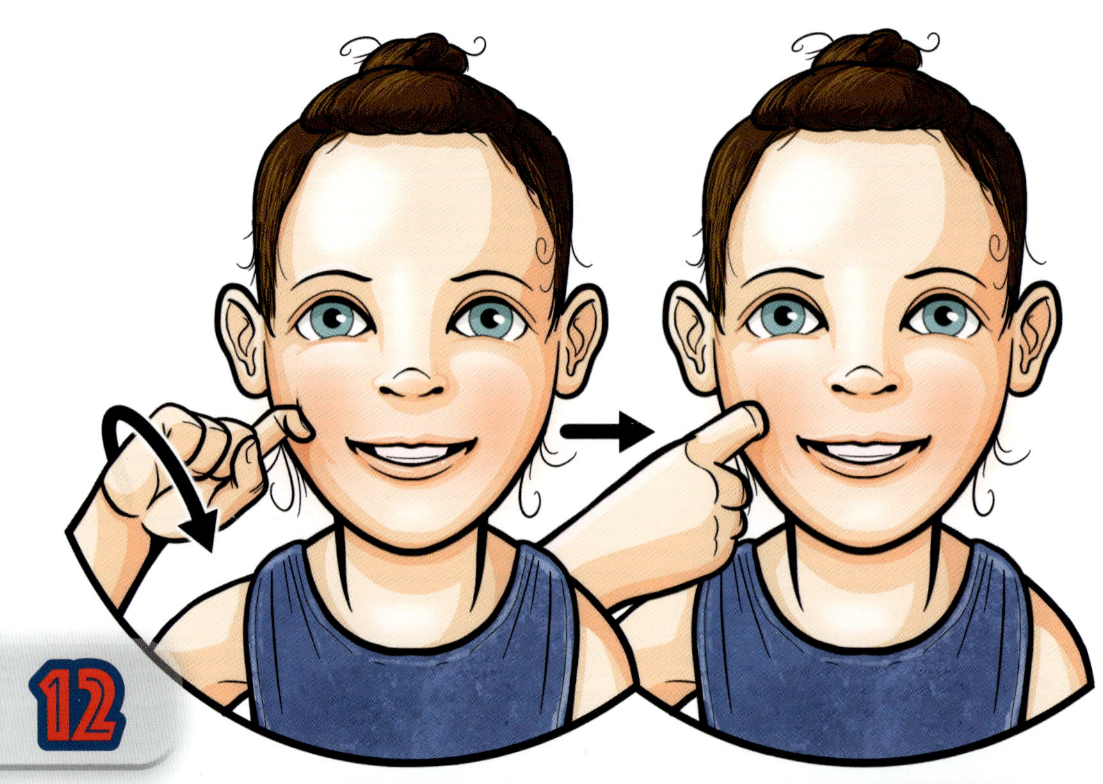

banana

cookie

egg

corn

(x2)

pizza

Published in 2025 by The Rosen Publishing Group, Inc.
2544 Clinton Street, Buffalo, NY 14224

First Edition

Special thanks to Michelle Rose, M.S., American Sign Language Consultant

Book Design: Tanya Dellaccio Keeney
Illustrator: Brad Manker, 35 Corks Art Studio

Photo Credits: Cover (background pattern) Olgastocker/Shutterstock.com; cover (girl) Pixel-Shot/Shutterstock.com; p. 3 Oksana Kuzmina/Shutterstock.com; p. 5 TimeImage Production/Shutterstock.com; p. 7 Africa Studio/Shutterstock.com; p. 9 Pair Srinrat/Shutterstock.com; p. 11 Pressmaster/Shutterstock.com; p. 13 Pashkovska Tetyana/Shutterstock.com; p. 15 matka_Wariatka/Shutterstock.com; p. 17 Prostock-studio/Shutterstock.com; p. 19 I AM NIKOM/Shutterstock.com; p. 21 Cookie Studio/Shutterstock.com; p. 23 feelartfeelant/Shutterstock.com.

Library of Congress Cataloging-in-Publication Data

Names: Davis, Raymie, author.
Title: Food / Raymie Davis.
Description: Buffalo, NY : PowerKids Press, [2024] | Series: Let's learn American Sign Language
Identifiers: LCCN 2023036621 (print) | LCCN 2023036622 (ebook) | ISBN 9781499443547 (library binding) | ISBN 9781499443530 (paperback) | ISBN 9781499443554 (ebook)
Subjects: LCSH: American Sign Language--Juvenile literature. | Food--Juvenile literature.
Classification: LCC HV2476 .D385 2024 (print) | LCC HV2476 (ebook) | DDC 419/.7--dc23/eng/20231106
LC record available at https://lccn.loc.gov/2023036621
LC ebook record available at https://lccn.loc.gov/2023036622

Manufactured in the United States of America

CPSIA Compliance Information: Batch #CSPK25. For further information contact Rosen Publishing at 1-800-237-9932.